Change Your Habits, Change Your Life in 21 Days

21-DAY CHALLENGE TO IMPROVE YOUR LIFE

By

PAUL GOLEMAN

TABLE OF CONTENTS

INTRODUCTION

I want to thank you and congratulate you for getting *Change Your Habits, Change Your Life in 21 Days: 21-Day Challenge to Improve Your Life.*

This book contains proven steps and strategies on how to change your life for the better through altering your habits.

Have you ever wanted to change your life for the better but had no idea where to get started? Do you look at other people and wonder how they have so much success while you are struggling to stay afloat? If so, it is time for you to find out how you can improve your sense of self and your ability to achieve your goals.

For some, it can be very hard to make realistic goals and reach them. You might want to live the kind of life you have always desired, but have no clear-cut path to help you get there. That is where changing your habits comes in

With this guide, you will learn everything you need to know about making each habit work for you. You will begin from the ground up, learning what makes habits form and how you can tell the difference between good and bad behaviors. You will even be taught how to uncover the deeper cause behind your bad habits, which can in turn help you break them for good.

After you have learned everything there is to know about habits, you will be challenged to try breaking bad ones and starting good ones for 21 days. It has often been said that it only takes 21 days to change your habits, and with this book, you will be given the opportunity to try just that. You will be guided throughout the challenge and given all the instructions you need to succeed.

When you practice good habits and get rid of bad ones, your life will improve almost right away. You will have more success in the workplace, and your home life will benefit too. This book is here to give you the tools you need to change your life in ways you never thought possible. Thanks again, I hope you enjoy it

CHAPTER ONE

WHAT ARE HABITS?

Habits are, most simply, the things we do when we don't always realize we're doing them. We get into the same routine of performing these tasks or actions, and after a while, they become second nature to us. For example, when you brush your teeth every morning, you probably always pick up your toothbrush with the same hand. There's no reason for this, and your life wouldn't be that much different if you used a different hand for a couple of days. But you don't, because you're already in the habit of using one over the other.

Of course, there are a lot of different types of habits, some of which are more significant than others. Good habits are harder to start than bad ones, and bad habits are harder to break than good ones. As human beings, we have the unique ability to try to determine which of our habits are good, and which ones are bad.

What Causes Habits To Form?

To start a habit, you first have to do the activity or perform the task that will eventually turn into a habit. Let's think about a usual morning routine to find an example. Jackie starts her day every morning by getting up and turning on the coffee maker before she goes back to her room to get ready for work. She pours her cup of coffee after getting dressed, since the coffee has had time to brew while she was preparing for her day.

Jackie never would have started this habit in the first place if she hadn't woken up one day and thought, "Wouldn't it be easier to make the coffee first?" That day, she tried it out, and ever since then she's been doing it the same way.

The more you repeat an activity or behavior, the more likely it is to become ingrained as a habit. Habits have three distinct aspects known as the cue, behavior, and reward. The cue is what makes you think of the habit, while the behavior is the habit itself. The reward is what you get, or feel like you get, from completing the action.

In Jackie's example, her alarm clock and waking up for the day is her cue. Turning on the coffee maker first is her behavior, and a more convenient cup of coffee is her reward.

How can I tell if a habit is bad or good?

Sometimes it can be very hard to tell if a habit is bad, good, or even neutral. Jackie's coffee maker habit seems pretty neutral, and as long as coffee every morning isn't causing any problems for her health, it's a fairly safe habit for her to continue. If, however, she finds out later in life that the caffeine is causing some harm, this might turn into a bad habit quickly. Since caffeine is an addictive substance, there are already some elements of a bad habit creeping into Jackie's morning ritual.

For the most part, if a habit isn't causing harm to you, your lifestyle, or the people around you, then it probably isn't bad. Smoking is a bad habit because it is bad for your health and can cause health and discomfort issues in others too. Biting your nails is a bad habit, because it damages your body and shows signs that you are nervous about something. On the other hand, eating a piece of fresh fruit every day is a good habit, since fruit is healthy and nutritious.

It's easy to figure out which habits are bad and which ones are good, but it can be harder to tell what makes bad habits happen in the first place.

How Can I Discover The Cause Of My Bad Habits?

Since every habit has a cue, even bad habits have to have a reason. Sometimes, you might not always know what causes your bad habits, but it's important to examine yourself and try to understand what makes you tick.

Let's consider Tom, who always eats a snack every time he sits down to watch a movie. Tom likes movies, and he likes snacks, so it makes sense that they go hand-in-hand with him. Unfortunately, all that snacking is making Tom's body less healthy, and he needs to stop.

There could be many reasons why Tom developed a snacking behavior with the cue of watching movies. Maybe he remembers being a kid, when he was allowed to eat popcorn when he saw movies. On the other hand, maybe he's supposed to be on a diet, but considers watching movies a time when he can cheat. He might even subtly associate snacking with movies just from all the times he's been to the theater, surrounded by candy bars. When he can figure out the cause of his bad habit, he can get closer to getting rid of it.

Is It Hard To Learn Good Habits?

Every habit is learned the same way. Whether a habit is good or bad, it comes from a cue that leads to a behavior that makes you feel rewarded in some way. Establishing good habits is just as easy as starting bad habits, but you might not think so at first. When you have a bad habit, it seems like your rewards are much better. You enjoy an off-limits snack like Tom, or you get some other benefit out of indulging in something you shouldn't do.

This is why it is so important to give yourself rewards for starting good habits, too. Do you forget to clean your house often, causing it to get messy and shabby-looking quickly? If so, you need to start developing a good habit of cleaning a little bit every week. Reward yourself with a little extra free time after cleaning to watch your favorite TV show or work on reading a book you love. When you get something out of it, good habits are a lot easier to start and to maintain.

CHAPTER TWO

HOW TO BREAK BAD HABITS

Breaking bad habits can be easy when you go into the task armed with the right information. There are tons of different ways you can work on improving your bad habits and replacing them with good ones instead. Some methods might work better for you than others, so don't be afraid to try a little bit of everything to see what keeps you on the right path to success. In no time, you'll start seeing some impressive changes in your life, all thanks to your attention to your bad habits.

Set realistic goals

First and foremost, set realistic goals for yourself. Every bad habit has to be broken down into stages, and it's important to work in small steps before you try to jump into the bigger picture. Remember that bad habits have cues, behaviors, and rewards, and try to break each one of your habits into these categories to figure out where to get started.

Rebecca is a nail-biter. She's been biting her nails since she was in the first grade, and now that she's in her thirties, she's ready to have healthy fingernails for once in her life. Unfortunately, this bad habit is so ingrained in her psyche that she doesn't know how to get started.

Rebecca can tell that the cue that causes her to bite her nails is her nervousness, and the reward is the sense that she's in control of something when she chews on her fingernails. Her first goal should be to find some other way of feeling in control, like holding a worry stone instead. After that, she can break her habit down into smaller steps, and slowly work toward growing her fingernails out long and healthy again.

Stay focused

Keep focused on your goals every step of the way to fight off your bad habits successfully. If you lose focus, you'll be back at square one in no time, and you'll have to start all over again.

Rebecca, for example, would have to start growing her fingernails from the ground up if she lost focus and started biting them again. If this happens, don't let yourself get discouraged. Just dust yourself off, get up, and try again.

Work with a friend or family member

Having a "bad habit buddy" can work wonders for keeping you accountable on your journey to breaking these behaviors. If you have a trusted friend or family member, ask them if they'll be your partner and maybe even try to break a few of their bad habits, too. When you work with someone, it's much easier to be happy about your accomplished goals, and to question yourself before sliding into a setback.

Rebecca's sister Maria is trying to stop spending too much money on clothes, shoes, and other unnecessary items every month. The two of them work together to break their bad habits by offering support when needed and sharing in each other's triumphs. They talk twice a week about how things are going, and it's a huge help to both of them.

Keep a record

Write down how things go every time you work on breaking your bad habit. It's a good idea to keep a chart listing out each day of the week and specifying your strengths, weaknesses, and new goals. This way, if you ever feel discouraged, you can look back over your notes and see how far you've come.

As Rebecca has worked on her nail-biting habit, she's kept notes on her goals and achievements. She also writes down every time something makes her nervous enough to want to bite her nails again. When she finally grew them out long enough to paint them for the first time in years, she wrote that down, too. Now she can look back on her progress and notice patterns of ups and downs.

Forgive yourself for mistakes

Everybody makes mistakes! It's okay if you make mistakes along the way. Some bad habits are a lot easier to break than others, and if you struggle for a long time with your worst ones, there's no shame in that. Smoking is a bad habit that can sometimes take years to stop, and even then, it's always tempting to backslide. If you find yourself making mistakes frequently, you might want to change tracks and come at your bad habits from a different angle.

Mistakes every now and then, however, are nothing more than chances to learn about what works and what doesn't.

Rebecca's first mistake in trying to quit biting her nails made her want to give up for good. She had been doing well, and had gone almost a whole week without biting. Then one night, she couldn't reach her sister on the phone at their usual time. She got worried about her sister and started biting her nails again. Only after her sister called her and said everything was fine did Rebecca realize she'd been biting. This setback was tough, since it made Rebecca feel like her progress had been for nothing. She reminded herself, however, that mistakes happen, and she kept pushing forward once again.

Try meditation

Meditation is a great way to work on breaking bad habits. When you meditate, you strengthen your mind and your willpower, and give yourself the ability to take control over your thoughts and actions. Even the worst of bad habits can be overcome with simple meditation techniques.

If you've never meditated before, don't worry! It's not too hard, especially with practice. Try an easy breathing meditation to get yourself in the right frame of mind. Follow these steps and you'll be meditating like a pro in no time:

- Sit down with your back straight and your eyes closed in a quiet place with no distractions.

- Set a timer for 5 or 10 minutes to begin with.

- Keeping your eyes closed, breathe at your normal rate.

- There's no need to slow down your breathing for this exercise.

- Count your breaths as your chest moves up and down.

- Count one in, one out; two in, two out, and so on.

- As you count, try to think of nothing but your breaths. If other thoughts come into your mind, push them away and keep your thoughts clear and free.

If you lose your place counting because you get distracted, start over.

It's okay if you can't concentrate all the way to ten breaths the first time you practice. It takes time to keep your mind clear. The more you work on this, the easier it will become to focus your thoughts and control your mind.

CHAPTER THREE

HOW CAN HABITS CHANGE MY LIFE?

Habits can do so much to change your life. When you practice regular good habits, you're sure to see your life improving almost instantly. You will be more successful, and you will have more time to enjoy your favorite hobbies and activities as well. You might even find that you have a new purpose in life when you get through the fog of bad habits.

On the other hand, bad habits can cause more trouble that they're worth, especially in the long run. They can make you feel stressed, and can even lead to problems like obsessive-compulsive disorder in some cases. In order to make the most out of your life, you need to remove bad habits and concentrate on the good ones.

Breaking bad habits can cut back on stress

When you get rid of bad habits, you're ready to live a more stress-free lifestyle. Having bad habits can make you feel overwhelmed, especially when they take control of your life. You might feel like you need to perform your bad habit rituals on a regular basis, and you might not be able to stop them if you only try halfheartedly. Many bad habits that involve some sort of harm or damage to your body add to your stress even more, as you find more and more reasons to worry about your health.

Cut back on your bad habits to reduce the amount of stress in your life. The more bad habits you break, the freer you will feel, and the better off your will be emotionally. You will have less to worry about overall, and you will have more to feel good about every time you put another bad habit behind you.

Breaking bad habits can help you feel happier

Much like reducing your stress levels, breaking bad habits can make you feel better overall as well. Having a lot of bad habits is emotionally exhausting. It wears you down, and it makes you think you will never be able to come through the other side to a life filled with only good habits. It is important to remember that you are always able to try again, no matter what might have happened in the past, and that you will be able to find happiness with fewer bad habits in your life.

Some bad habits are serious enough to lead you toward depression and anxiety. In these situations, you might be on the road toward obsessive-compulsive disorder, or you might have other mental health issues you need to think about. The sooner you are able to stop repeating these bad habits, the happier you will be in the long run. Remember that no bad habit is so great that you cannot get beyond it with a little effort and planning.

Breaking bad habits can give you more time for activities you enjoy

Do you spend a lot of time smoking? Do you stop in the middle of your favorite TV shows to get up and find a snack? Are you often out of time to spend with your family because you waste time procrastinating instead? Every bad habit takes time out of your life that you could spend doing something else you enjoy more. There is no reason you need to spend so much time on your bad habits, and when you learn to break them, you have a lot more free time to spend however you choose.

Take Brendan for example. Brendan is a smoker, and he has been for most of his life. Every time he goes out with his family or friends, he has to stop in the middle of whatever he's doing and go have a smoke. Sometimes, he even leaves movie theaters or dinner dates to step outside for a cigarette. If Brendan could break this bad habit, he'd be able to spend more of his time with the people he enjoys being with, instead of standing alone outside smoking.

Starting good habits can help you succeed in life

Did you know that good habits can help you get ahead in life? When you have good habits to back you up, you can get a lot done in the workplace and around the house as well. More free time means you'll have more energy and mental stamina to devote to the things you need to get accomplished, and with good habits, you'll learn how to be better prepared for just about anything life can throw at you.

Let's look at Brendan again for this example. Smoking is a bad habit, but if he could stop smoking and replace that with a good habit, he might really improve his work. One good habit is reading a little bit every day and trying to learn something new. If Brendan takes the time he used to spend on smoke breaks reading and learning instead, he'll have more knowledge to help him succeed at work.

Starting good habits can get you organized

Good habits are great for helping you stay organized, as long as you don't go over the top with them. There are tons of different good habits that can help you get your life in order, like cleaning frequently, keeping track of your budget, planning family events on a calendar, and more. Keeping lists is another good habit to get into, especially when you frequently forget things or run late to your appointments.

Don't let keeping lists and making plans take the place of a bad habit in your life, however! If you get too worried about sticking to your plans, you'll wind up making yourself upset instead of using this skill for good. It's easy to fall into the trap of thinking negatively about your lists and calendars, so don't overdo it. Spend just a couple of minutes a day getting organized so you don't let it overtake your life.

Starting good habits can help you find a cause or goal in life

Finally, good habits can lead to something even greater if you give them a chance to. Maybe you spend a lot of time reading and learning, and you eventually learn about a cause that piques your interest. You might go from that into volunteering for a local branch of some support group, and from there, you may even find a new calling in life. Who knows? Your good habits give you plenty of chances to do something great with your life.

Samantha found out about her true calling in much the same way. When she was trying to educate herself on local organizations, she found out about one that helps terminally ill children take their dream vacations. She started volunteering, and in a few years, she was offered a job by the same group. She never expected her life to take that kind of turn, but she's never looked back since.

CHAPTER FOUR

MILLIONAIRE HABITS

Who doesn't have dreams of being a millionaire? We all wish we could get to that point in life, and some people actually make it. Of course, there are always going to be millionaires that get where they are because their family has money, but that isn't the case in every situation. A lot of millionaires these days are self-made, and there's no reason you can't be the same way.

When you practice millionaire habits, you're giving yourself plenty of opportunity to earn a lot of money and succeed in life without having to make difficult changes to do it. Millionaire habits are a little tougher to enforce than normal, everyday good habits, but when you spend time working on them, you'll see the results quickly.

What makes a millionaire habit?

Millionaire habits are the good behaviors you can add into your daily routine to help you make the most out of life. Millionaires often earn their money the hard way, and self-made millionaires are getting more and more common in modern society. When you practice these habits, you can work your way up the economic ladder too. You'll see changes in no time, and you'll be on your way toward being a self-made millionaire yourself.

So what makes these habits so different from any others? They're all good habits, and they're all designed to help you improve yourself in some way. Money isn't everything, and you can't expect to go out into the world and make money without first improving yourself as a person. The more you do to work on yourself, the better off you'll be in the workplace and in the rest of your life, too.

Read often and learn as much as you can

Being well-read is the first step toward a better life. If you set aside half an hour every day to read something, you'll learn more about how to communicate with others both verbally and in writing. You'll discover words you've never encountered before, and you will have more to talk about with the people you work with too. Reading anything is good practice for communication, but try to read novels instead of magazines or web sites whenever possible to get the best results.

Try to learn something new every week, too. Even if it's something you'll never use again, look up a topic and see what you can find out about it. You might not ever need to know how to use a water softener, for example, but it might be interesting to find out what they do! You never know when this new information will come in handy down the line.

Stay up to date on current information

Current information is always important, and it's a great way to break the ice and do some networking in a work environment. Current events don't always have to be political or even that important, but it's a good idea to pay attention to these as well. You can also pepper your reading with fun things like the latest celebrity gossip, to give yourself an in with just about any conversation

Make lists

We've already talked about the importance of making lists in general, but when it comes to working toward becoming a self-made millionaire, lists are crucial. You can't become successful without keeping track of your work, your finances, and your time, so be sure to handle your lists in the most organized fashion possible to stay on top of everything.

Use separate notebooks and differently-colored highlighters or pens to keep track of different parts of your life. Keep a calendar with plenty of notes, so you never forget when important deadlines are coming up. It's also a good idea to list out contacts that can help you get ahead in the workplace, and keep them on hand for those times when you need to do a little extra networking.

Be careful with your finances

Plan your finances carefully to put your money to work for you. Don't spend all over the place, and plan a budget that you can follow. It's important not to stretch your budget so thin that it's impossible to stick to it for even a single month, but to keep from giving yourself too much wiggle room as well. When you plan out your budget carefully and pay attention to your finances, you'll find it much easier to put aside money in the long run.

Spread your money throughout many different areas as well. If you can make money in more than one way, by all means, do it! You can hold down a regular job and work on something else on the side, such as selling crafts online or baked goods locally. Be sure to put some money in savings and try some in stocks as well. The more you spread your finances, the more return you will eventually see. It will take time and patience, but you will be a self-made millionaire eventually when you stick to these great habits.

CHAPTER FIVE

21-DAY CHALLENGE

Supposedly, it takes 21 days to break an old habit or start a new one. Are you ready for a challenge? Take this 21-day challenge to help kick bad habits for good. You'll be ready to face anything when you get through with these three weeks, and you'll have a lot less bad habits to worry about too. You're sure to see results right away when you get started on this challenge, so pick a day and get ready to change your life for the better.

Day one

Write down your ultimate goal in big letters on a note card and keep it close to you. Put it in your purse or pocket, or place it next to your computer screen at work.

Day two

Choose a reward that will help you either break your bad habit or start your good one. Make sure the reward isn't detrimental, like an extra snack if you're trying to diet.

Day three

Set smaller goals for yourself. Plan out steps along the way to help you reach your goals more easily.

Day four

If you haven't started a journal already, do so now. Write down how things have been going, and try to make a few quick notes every day.

Day five

Practice focusing on your ultimate goal. Write down what will be better about your life when you can make changes in your habits for the better.

Day six

If you're breaking a bad habit, pick something to do in place of that habit, like reading a little bit every day. If you're starting a good habit, take this day to reinforce the reasons why this habit is a good idea for you.

Day seven

Time for your first check-in! How have you been doing? Have you slipped up and repeated your bad habit or forgotten to practice your good one? Write all this down in your journal.

Day eight

Find a friend to help you keep accountable as you work toward your ultimate goal. Ask someone to let you check in every day and report how you're doing.

Day nine

Reward yourself! You've completed several days of your challenge now. If you've made a few mistakes, it's okay. You still deserve a reward.

Day ten

Start practicing meditation. Try a breathing meditation for 5 minutes today, and keep notes on how well it goes for you.

Day eleven

Write down all the mistakes you've made on your journey. Think about them, and how you could do things differently to avoid those mistakes in the future. Forgive yourself and move on.

Day twelve

Meditate again today. This time, try it for 10 minutes, and once again keep track of how it works for you. If you notice some changes you'd like to make, write those down too.

Day thirteen

Check in with your habit buddy and let them know how well you're doing. Be sure to express how important this is, and to tell them the good as well as the bad.

Day fourteen

It's time for your second check-in! How are things going now? Have mistakes been less frequent? Is the habit getting easier? Write all of this down in your journal.

Day fifteen

Reward yourself again! Don't go too long in between giving yourself some rewards, or you'll feel like you aren't getting anything out of your new habit regime.

Day sixteen

Schedule a 10-minute meditation session. If it's going really well, try it for 15 or even 20 minutes instead.

Day seventeen

Make a couple of lists to organize your thoughts. Make a list of pros with breaking your habit or starting your new one, and cons too. This will help you find out what's easy and what you might still need to work on in the future.

Day eighteen

Write down some thoughts on how your life has changed since you started your journey. You might also write notes on how you think it will go in the future after you finish your challenge too.

Day nineteen

Check off all the goals you've accomplished along your journey. You're so close to the end now, and it is important to see how far you've come.

Day twenty

Things should be getting easier by now. Check in with your habit buddy one more time to let them know how your challenge has gone.

Day twenty-one

You've reached the end of your challenge. Congratulations! Now your good habit should be deeply ingrained in your psyche, and your bad habit should be long gone.

CONCLUSION

So where can you go from here? You've learned a lot about what makes habits form, and how to tell a good habit from a bad one. You've even learned how to replace your bad habits with good ones, and how to make them work for you. You know how to start on your path to becoming a self-made millionaire, and you've even been given a 21-day habit-changing challenge to help you get started. With all this excellent information, you're ready to get out there and make a difference in your life, one habit at a time.

So what are you waiting for? You've got what you need to get started. All you have to do now is pick a bad habit you want to change or choose a good habit you want to start, and work through the 21-day challenge. In no time, you'll see differences in your work, your home life, and your overall emotional well-being.

You owe it to yourself to practice good habits!

ABOUT THE AUTHOR

Hi, I'm **Paul**, and here's a little about me:

I'm an entrepreneur, internet marketer, author, life coach, professional speaker, fitness enthusiast, and world traveler. I feel extremely blessed for the life that I live.

I bring seven years of niche expertise in self-help and personal development. I'm a business management graduate and I like to study people who appear to be unbeatable against all odds or challenges of life. I seek answers for failures and lack of growth, and thus I want to help people reinvent themselves. I believe this: Each and every person is the sole controller of his/her life. If you do not take the utmost care of your life, no one else will.

One Last Thing...

If you enjoyed this book or found it useful I'd be very grateful if you'd post a short review on Amazon. Your support really does make a difference, and I read all the reviews personally so I can get your feedback and make this book even better.

Thanks again for your support!